Someone Like Me

PATRICIA MacLACHLAN

Illustrations by
CHRIS SHEBAN

A NEAL PORTER BOOK
ROARING BROOK PRESS
NEW YORK

*For my grandchildren Sofia, Ella, Nicholas, Anna, Harry,
and Lucy—and for all children who are living the life
now that they may write about one day. —P.M.*

Text copyright © 2017 by Patricia MacLachlan
Illustrations copyright © 2017 by Chris Sheban
A Neal Porter Book
Published by Roaring Brook Press
Roaring Brook Press is a division of Holtzbrinck Publishing
Holdings Limited Partnership
175 Fifth Avenue, New York, New York 10010
The art for this book was created using watercolor, colored pencil, and graphite.
mackids.com

Library of Congress Control Number: 2016038433

ISBN: 978-1-62672-334-4

Our books may be purchased in bulk for promotional, educational, or business use. Please
contact your local bookseller or the Macmillan Corporate and Premium Sales Department
at (800) 221-7945 ext. 5442 or by e-mail at MacmillanSpecialMarkets@macmillan.com.

First edition 2017
Printed in China by RR Donnelley Asia Printing Solutions Ltd., Dongguan City, Guangdong Province
10 9 8 7 6 5 4 3 2 1

If you were a little girl
who listened to stories

over and over

and over—

Jack the horse and twelve cows
broke through the fence and
walked all the way to town,

Aunt Emma's dog with
three names—

Tommy,

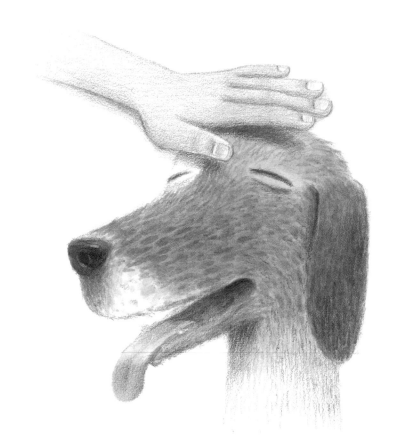

Rascal,

and Come Along

If you were a little girl who read books
every night,

every day,

walking home from the library,
reading as her mother
led her across streets

A girl who hid under the flowered
tablecloth of the dinner table,
watching the shoes
of the grown-ups who told secrets

and never knew
she was there,

who tried to teach her dog to talk
by moving his lips like hers

and her chicken's beak, too,

and loved climbing the cottonwood tree,
watching the sky that flew above her,

and who ran away once

with a little boy who told her he'd find her
a white horse,

and didn't.

And followed people,
listening to their talk
and their songs
and how they laughed . . .

If you were a girl whose great-grandmother loved
the smell and feel of prairie earth,

and ran through the grasses
sending the geese on the slough to
fly up

around

and back again

Then maybe you would grow up to be
someone who carries small bags of sweet prairie earth,

someone who writes about how the sky looks
through the branches of trees,

geese against the clouds,
and writes about talking dogs
and chickens who scratch stories in the dirt

and a white horse to ride
through dreams,
you might be
someone like me.

A writer.